MW01069194

GOOD GOLLY MISS HOLLY

by Linda Bower Johnson

RoseDog Books

PITTSBURGH, PENNSYLVANIA 15238

RoseDog Books
585 Alpha Drive, Suite 103
Pittsburgh, PA 15238
Visit our website at *www.rosedogbookstore.com*

ISBN: 978-1-63867-400-9
eISBN: 978-1-63867-501-3

This book is dedicated to my brothers and sisters—you will never know how much I love and appreciate all you have done for me.

Jo Anne Bower Schmauss and Robert Schmauss
Harry Lee Bower, Sr. and Patty Bower
Frances Bower Counts and Johnny Counts
Margaret Bower Ackley and Sam Ackley
Ben Bower and Liann Bower
June Bower Putnam and Kelvin Putnam
Charles Bower and Tami Bower

Picture taken with our parents, September 1953 at our home in the country that burned in 1954.

One of the last pictures taken of the Bower Children (June 2012)
Top left to right: Charlie, Ben and Harry Lee
Bottom left to right: Frances, Maggie, Juni, Jo Anne and Linda

Preface

I have had this book on my mind since the loss of my precious dog, Holly Belle, in 2011. She was so funny, loveable and just brought our dysfunctional family together. We all loved her so, and I thought that must be how grandchildren are—they bring you together because everyone loves them. Anyway, as I started putting my thoughts together, I remembered more of my pets, and I felt the love of animals had a beginning at an early age, and so the title is "Good Golly Miss Holly" but this book includes all our family pets through the years. During the pandemic of 2020, my sister, Frances, asked me to please finish the book so she could read it before we all passed away. I realize many young people won't even understand some of the terms and ideas in this book, but anyone over 60 should enjoy, so here we go…

Nephew Kenny, Aunt Linda and Uncle Charlie

Being the youngest of eight children, I was blessed with parents who didn't care what kind of pets or how many we had. My earliest memory of a pet was a black Cocker Spaniel named Ginger. Our house in a rural area had burned down when I was five and we moved to a small town in Ohio—Frankfort. Frankfort had a population of 1000 and still does. I thought I was in the big city and taught my nephew, who was three, how to walk on the edges of the street curbs like we were in the circus on a tightrope until my Dad caught me and yelled at me for teaching him such a dangerous thing. All traffic on Route US 35 from Chillicothe to Dayton went by our house on Main Street. My nephew, Kenny, was like my little brother and often stayed with us since he was my parents' first grandchild. We would fuss over Mom's attention, he saying "She's my Grandma" and me saying, "She's my Mommy". Anyway, we learned the sad lesson of losing a beloved pet early in life when we were crossing the street with my Mom, and Ginger ran out ahead of us. She was hit by a car driven by an elderly man who was quite upset. It didn't help that my nephew screamed, "I hate you, old man, I hate you!"

I started school at six and soon was reading in the Airplane Group. There were airplanes, trains and cars—how sad to be a car! Our books had the old characters like Dick, Jane, etc. and Tag was a dog in one of the books. Enter a dog that just "came to our house" and we named him Tag. He was a mixed breed but was very pretty, black and white and of medium size. He loved chasing cars, chasing cats, and anyone not in the family. He would follow us to school, and during summer at Bible School in the Methodist Church, the doors were open (no air conditioning then), he came to the two big front doors sniffing and I was praying, "Please don't let him come in!" Once Daddy took Tag away to a better place because he was always barking and trying to get after people other than family. My sister Frances (who was married and lived about 12 miles away) said Tag came to their home. She brought him back to a home full of thankful kids, and my Dad was so proud that he found his way to her house, he let him stay.

Even though my Mom explained the birds and the bees to me (because I had seen Tag in the act and thought he and the female dog were "stuck" together), she said that animals mated only because of nature and not because they liked it. I caught sight of Tag "mating" again and told my Mom at the dinner table that she was wrong because I saw Tag and he was enjoying it because he was smiling. This was not amusing to my parents, but my brothers and sisters laughed and laughed!

Tag became an inside dog and with five of the eight children still living at home, he was "our" dog. My youngest brother, Charlie, and I teased him and taught him to jump high in the air after Mom's throw pillows which we threw. He would show his gums and say, "Rah, rah Frankfort!" as my sisters, Juni and Maggie, were cheerleaders and that was a school cheer we were all used to saying. My future brother-in-law, Sam, would pick up my sister to take her to school. He always had Dentine Chewing Gum and would give each of us siblings a piece and Tag would always get one too! Once when we were gone from home, but Tag was there, my married brother, Harry Lee, came. We never locked doors back then, and he thought it would be fun to act like he was stealing something and see what Tag did. Well, he had a scar on his stomach until the day he died from Tag attacking him for putting empty pop bottles under his coat! Harry Lee and is wife Patty had a boxer named "Rocky"! This was way before the Rocky movies. Rocky was a good dog but annoying because of all the saliva always drooling from his mouth. Once for a big family dinner, Harry Lee brought Rocky and in the middle of the dinner, Tag and Rocky went for a knock-out battle underneath the dinner table. There was never a dull moment at our house.

My Dad won a Catholic Church raffle for $1000 when I was eight. For the first time in their married life, my parents were able to buy their own home. It was on Second Street right behind our house that we rented on Main. After we moved there, Tag and I would go sit on the front porch of our "first" house because we liked it better. It took a while to adjust to the "new house". My Dad was a smoker and didn't sleep well at night. I have memories of him sitting in his chair in the living room in the middle of the night with just the light from his cigarette showing and Tag sitting by his side.

Tag loved my Mother more than anyone. Mom never learned to drive and she walked everywhere. When she returned home from the Post Office, Grocery or visiting, he would jump and jump to welcome her home. When my brother Charlie next to me in age (two years older) was in trouble my Mom would spank him, but first she had to catch him. He always ran, usually laughing the whole time. He would usually get under my parents' high, four-poster bed with plenty of room underneath. Tag would always get into the act by biting Charlie—we always said this had to do with Charlie catching Tag's tail in the door accidently, and Tag never forgot! No matter who fought in our family (imagine five kids ages 5-14), Tag always was against Charlie and would bite him! Charlie had his own dog, a little all-black mutt, again who "came to our house". Charlie called her Ring from a previous dog the family had before I was born or could remember. Anyway, Ring and Tag got along fine. I liked Ring because I could dress her in doll clothes. Once I was setting out for a walk with Ring dressed real nicely and Charlie came by on his bike, ripped Ring from my hands and threw the clothes off! I still dressed her up when he was out playing!

Tag never liked anyone other than the family and barked and scared people. He barked if people knocked on the door, barked if people walked down the alley—Tag barked a lot. He was our family dog, and as each child married or left home—one brother, Ben, to the Air Force and Viet Nam, two sisters Maggie and Juni, married, and Charlie married and went to the Army and also Viet Nam, Tag became more and more my dog. After I graduated, I went to secretarial school in Columbus, Ohio, which was only about 50 miles away, but I was so homesick I would come home every weekend. One Friday evening, my Mom was crying and told me to eat my supper and after I ate, she had something to tell me. Of course, I couldn't eat until she told me that she had to have Tag put to sleep. He had been our dog for 12 plus years and he wasn't a puppy when he came to our house, so we didn't know how old he was but I was very mad and mean about the whole thing and accused she and Daddy of having him put down so they could go to Florida to visit my oldest sister, Jo Anne. I was even madder when they came home with a beagle puppy named "Teddy" which my brother-in-law, Bob, had given them in Florida. Teddy even flew home on an airplane! I never liked that dog. My Dad would walk to a brother-in-law's service station (it was a small town, that is

Mom, Dad and Tag

Mom and Tag

Tag and Ring

Me, Mom and Tag

Mom, Stephanie and Tag

Teddy with Mom, nephew Mike, niece Christina and niece Jill

He loved the food and attention!

what people did) to hang out and he would bring his "boy" a candy bar every evening. Now they say how dangerous chocolate is for dogs, but Teddy waited by the fence every evening for his candy bar. Teddy was a fat dog! When Daddy got sick and was dying of lung cancer, he would whisper to me when I left the hospital, "get the boy a candy bar" and I would do so and stand outside the fence crying while "the boy" ate his candy bar. Our Daddy died and Mom, Teddy and I lived on. I decided to move to Florida so Mom and Teddy were left alone. Mom decided to sell the house and move to an apartment so my sister Frances and brother Harry Lee took Teddy "away". They never told any of us where he went, but Mom loved living in her new apartment and they didn't allow pets. She went on Senior Citizen trips and didn't have to worry about leaving a pet behind.

Fast forward several years, and I married. The man I married had a German Shepherd dog named "Joy". Joy was very shy. But she also followed the call of nature and several months after we married, she delivered about five puppies. They were very cute and since we lived in an apartment and Joy lived with Jim's mother in the country, we gave them all away. Later, Jim and I bought land in the country and lived in a trailer until we could build our "dream home". Joy came to live with us and enjoyed my singing. She would howl along with me as I sang! She also loved riding in cars. Jim bought a jeep, and I would practice driving a shift (which I never had) and poor Joy would get in the jeep with me and slide from back to front as I tried to drive. I don't know why we didn't have her spayed, but she was in "heat" and we had erected a nice shed to keep tools, etc., in, and while we worked during the day, Jim would put Joy in the shed. I never saw him as mad as the day we came home from work, and a male dog left the shed!! He was like a father of a teenage girl. Joy had the sweetest puppies but they looked like Mexican Chihuahuas! They were easy to give away, and one went to a doctor I worked with who had little children. He said their puppy grew up with long legs and big body and cost them so much money, tearing things up, etc., but they loved it and couldn't give it away.

Meanwhile, while Mom would visit me in Florida, as I said she always walked everywhere since she never knew how to drive, she thought she would walk to the little store down the road and take Joy with her as protection since Jim and I were working. She told Joy to wait outside and knowing Mom she talked a great deal with the store clerk and when she came out, Joy was nowhere in sight. Mom walked back to our trailer and there was Joy sitting on the front porch like "what took you so long?" Since we lived out in the boonies, sometimes strangers would come to the door for direction, information, etc. Jim would goose Joy who just sat as they walked up so they could see she was a German Shepherd, but she never was a good watch dog. Joy also tried to get our approval by bringing things to the porch. One Easter, Mom was visiting, and looked out and said, "Joy has killed the Easter Bunny!" There on the porch was a dead rabbit. Joy also liked to get involved with other animals and as I said, she liked to get in the car. Once when we had a new Mustang, and were putting Mom's suitcase in the car to take her to the airport, Joy jumped in and spread the aroma of a skunk that she must have "played with". We had to drive to the airport with the windows down!

One Christmas, we went home to Mom and the family in Ohio. There was a black lab dog that had been running wild in Frankfort, and my sister Frances wanted Jim to see it. Jim fell in love with the dog, and since it didn't seem to have an owner, we flew back to Florida with it! Poor Joy! She was so jealous. Jim named the dog Mike and it would chase balls, run with Jim and while he did this, Joy would go to the side of the trailer and look around like nobody loved her. Did I tell you we lived out in the boonies? We had bought two acres of land to build our dream home, and there were people behind us who had cattle. One day when we were at work, Mike jumped the fence and tried to play with the cows. He "playfully" bit one cow's ear off, for which we had to pay. Sadly, Jim took Mike to a vet who said there were plenty of people who would adopt him, but he would tell them about the cow incident. Joy was our only dog again.

We lived during the time of the gas lines (early 70's), and Jim's job as a contract carpenter went downhill, so he decided to use the G.I. Bill and go to college. Back we moved to Tampa, so Joy went to live with Jim's Mother again. One evening his Mom came to town and we took her out to dinner and had a nice evening, and at the end of the evening, she told us Joy was dead, having been hit by a car. She, like my Mom, wanted us to enjoy our meal before hearing the sad news. I had liked Joy but Jim cried and cried and I felt bad that I didn't feel that sorry. By then, we were planning on having our own little baby and I had other things on my mind.

We had two little boys—the jewels of my life, and Jim had finished college and started working for the Army as an accountant. I was a "stay-at-home Mom" what I wanted to be my whole life! Life was good and we moved to Douglasville, Georgia, with a two-year-old and a six-month-old baby. I was so happy to be a stay-at-home Mom even though it was busy with two boys in diapers. One evening Jim brought home the biggest dog I had ever seen and said that the boys needed a pet. The dog would stand and put his front paws on my shoulders and was bigger than me. I cried and had a "Linda fit" and said that I couldn't protect myself from such a big dog, let alone our precious boys, so the dog went back to its owner. Not too long after

Joy's first set of babies

I loved them all and they were easy to give away

Jim and Mike

Mom playing with Joy

Joy enjoying our "country place"

Joy with her baby from her last litter

that Jim came home with a "puppy" which was so sweet and so not trained! One son would poop, the next one would poop and then the puppy would poop. I did get this puppy to the Vet for its first shots and was trying to deal with three poopy animals when my Mother-in-law, Frances, and her sister, Doris, came to visit. They just loved the puppy. They were on their way to Doris' home in North Carolina. She loved the puppy so much that I asked if she wanted to take it with her and she did! After she left, I remembered she didn't get its shot record, and Jim said, "people in rural North Carolina don't worry about a dog's shot records." I was back to only two poopy kids again!

The arrival of Duchess: Being without a dog didn't last long. Again, Jim came home with a beautiful, full-grown dog named Duchess. She was given to him by a work friend. Both boys adored her, and she stayed outside except on real cold nights when she slept in the garage or in her house with a light bulb inside. Jim took Duchess and the boys to the veterinarian to get all her records straight and came home furious. I asked if she acted up, and he said, "no the boys did!" They had run and jumped in the reception area. Being so close in age, what one didn't think of, the other did, and that is another book I am writing. Anyway, I was glad he wasn't mad at Duchess. The boys took to her right away and Joey would take his pre-school papers out to show Duchess. She was very smart. We had an acre lot all fenced in, but we would often see her come up the street from the other side of the subdivision. We watched to see if she jumped the fence which she did. She would jump on the roof of her doghouse and then over the fence to the neighbors behind us who had no fence. We moved her doghouse and it wasn't long before we caught her coming home from the other side of the neighborhood again. We watched her, and she would go into the drainage ditch in our side yard and walk the entire length of an underground water pipe to the end of the subdivision and get out there! She was just checking things out. She was big and red and hairy and some people were afraid of her but she was very gentle. I must admit I was not a good "Doggy Mom" in those days. After Thanksgiving dinner, I would give her the whole turkey carcass which she proudly carried all around the yard before devouring it, bones and all. When the kids were beyond day-care and stayed at home in the summer, I noticed that their tube socks were always so muddy and dirty but summed it up to boys being boys. One rainy day, I came home early and when I came in the house, there was Duchess wearing their socks on all four feet! I screamed and she ran upstairs, so I realized where the extra dirty socks were coming from. They were bringing her into the house when I wasn't there with socks on so she wouldn't dirty the carpets!

Duchess loved my husband and anything to which he paid attention. He made a very nice garden one summer and put railroad ties down to terrace the crops. He was very proud of his tomatoes. Before they were ripe, Duchess would pick them and place them on our deck—in a row! No teeth marks, and that was that.

The boys and Jim played with Duchess and I would feed her when necessary, but she wasn't one of my top priorities. Once Joey had come home and was in the back yard, and we weren't home. The neighbors' Chows (two) behind us had gotten loose and were in our yard. They terrorized Joey. When I got home and he was crying over being so scared, I asked him what Duchess had done, and he said, "she just ran away!" Once a chicken from the Spanish family behind us flew into our yard. They were so excited as Duchess tried to "play" with their chicken. The chicken was flying all over the place and they were screaming in Spanish! It was an exciting time and I, of course, thought it was funny. The chicken was caught, and peace returned to the neighborhood. Also, one day we were having a picnic in our back yard when a little kitten ran through. Duchess picked up the kitten and was throwing it in the air! We did get the kitten out of her mouth safely, and I (who loved cats more than dogs) never asked for a cat after that.

I returned to work and decided to work for the Army where Jim did so we could ride to work except he being in Management had to work over many times, and then we would drive separately. We were busy, the boys in soccer, tennis and running and time flew by. We were all getting older. One day when we returned from work, Joey came in crying, saying Duchess was in the ditch and just kept falling over. She would try to stand and would fall over. We took her to the Vet, and she was dying. She wasn't getting enough oxygen to live, and so the Vet had to put her down. What a crying group of men—Jim, the two boys and even the Vet! Jim built her a casket, and Joey put family pictures and her favorite toys in the casket. We buried her in the extra lot where she ran and played. The next day at work as I described the two boys hanging onto each other crying, one of my Army Officers said to remember that day as I would never see another one like that until I died! Yes, sometimes I worked with really sensitive people!

The boys grew and when they were 15 and 13, we sold our home and had a new home built. It was probably the worst time in the world to take on a bigger mortgage—Jim was working overtime as he had been promoted to a very stressful position—the kids were fully pledged teenagers. James. the oldest, had a part-time job from which I had to pick him up after I got home from work, and Joey, the youngest, was running track and had to be places after school. All that plus a-full-time working Mom who was premenopausal and trying to learn to cut and paste on a computer at work after having typed on a type-

Duchess

James, Joey and Duchess

Joey and Duchess
(She would help him find the eggs on Easter!)

Duchess

Duchess and James

Mom, Joey, James and Duchess
(Duchess was getting older as we all were!)

writer for 30 years and was ready to throw the new "computers" and herself out the window! I think we all hated each other!

Joey was turning 14! Since he was my baby and I wanted him happy, I thought about getting a new dog. He was excited about getting a Jack Russell dog—Frazier was on television at the time, and everyone loved the dog on the show named Eddie.

I would look at newspaper ads, and Jim would say, "No dog!" and then I would look some more.

Finally, I found an ad in our local newspaper for Jack Russell puppies that didn't cost an arm and a leg, and Joey and I went to the man's farm. There was the sweetest Momma dog standing up at the fence begging to be taken and on the ground were the prettiest "Jack Russell" puppies we had ever seen. Most of them were black and white or brown and white, but one stood out as being copper-colored and white. She was the one we selected. I could relate to the mother who wanted to escape! We had our dog! Many names came up like Copper, names of animals in the movies, but we settled on Holly! We had found our dog. We took her home. James, my oldest son, was still in bed and upset with me because he didn't get to go with friends the night before, but he forgot all about that when he saw Holly. Joey had a track meet that same day so I took him, and James and Jim were in charge of Holly. They fell in love immediately. We took her to the vet, Dr. Morgan, who proclaimed she wasn't a Jack Russell puppy but a Rat Terrier. I didn't like the sound of that so we continued calling her a Jack Russell Terrier. Now came the hard job—training her.

We bought a book on cage training which seemed easy. During the day while we were gone, we would put Holly in her cage. She never

Holly at 7 weeks

seemed to make a mess and was happy when we returned in the evening. One evening Jim and I returned to a poopy mess in the cage and on Holly. I am certain that James came home, played with her, probably fed her something and then rushed to his part-time job after putting her back in the cage without letting her potty. He denied this.

At bed time we would put Holly back in the cage. This is when we knew she could talk. She would scream and cry like a crazy woman, cussing all of us, sometimes making us all laugh. After several weeks of this, we decided she could sleep at the foot of our bed.

When James was a Senior, he had his own car and could drive himself and Joey to school. He was also feeling full of himself as Seniors often do. One time I came home to Holly smelling like a cigar! When confronted, he said that he had smoked a cigar outside and kissed her on the head. I always found out what that boy was doing!

Holly had a way to get James in trouble. He chose the basement bedroom in our new house to be away from the rest of us. One night after we were all in bed, Holly barked and barked. James was letting his friends in his window! Jim called to them and said, "Get up here!" and up the stairs marched his friends with filthy, muddy shoes on my new carpet! James had to clean it the next day. He said, "I hate you Holly!" I am sure we would have all slept through the night without her warning.

We didn't have Holly very long when she went into "heat". I never thought I would see the day when Jim Johnson would buy sanitary napkins for a dog, but he came home with a little leather outfit that you fit the pad into. It was really cute like bikini bottoms. I told him she needed a bra with it. Holly chewed it off! Anyway, she got out one day and there was a beautiful cocker spaniel out there and they would look through the door and cry for each other. I think she did get with him, but I wasn't certain. We took her to the veterinarian and I hated to think she would have an abortion, but when he spayed her, he said there were no babies. She had her hysterectomy, and what a pitiful little thing she was. She wouldn't eat or drink water. Both boys would carry water in their hands and try to get her to drink. She just sat on the sofa like a princess. I could never imagine them treating me that way if I were sick, but we all loved this little dog and would do anything for her.

My Mom was in her eighties now and would come to visit us for a month each year. When she first came, Holly fell in love with her. My Mom had a cough in her later years and would always carry a tissue around with her. Holly loved taking those tissues off Mom's lap and running with them. She would also jump up and take our napkins off our laps when we were eating. When my Mom went to bed, she would take her Vicks VapoRub and a smaller jar of lip balm along. The whole house would almost be asleep when Mom would call out, "Linda, Holly has my lip balm jar!" I would retrieve it, and Holly would wait until she thought we were asleep and do it over again. She also loved suit cases, and when my sister, Juni, visited once, Holly came from the guest room with Juni's cosmetics' bag from her suit case! She just wanted to look pretty!

One time when Mom flew in, she was just getting settled at the house when my oldest brother, Harry Lee, called to make sure Mom got there okay as she traveled by herself and the family worried until they knew I had picked her up and she was at my house. We were talking and I was telling him Mom was okay, when we heard, "Yelp, yelp, yelp!" from Holly. "What is going on there, Linda?" he asked. Mom

They were like teenagers who couldn't date each other!

had picked up Holly's bone-like dinosaur and had thrown it at Holly and hit her in the head! Mom said she thought it was a toy!

We tried to train Holly so she would go outside by herself and then come back to the door. This worked most times, unless she thought otherwise. One time she just ran from us into the woods, down the street, and the closer we would get to her, she just ran away. I was in the front yard pleading with her to come home, when my Mom came out on the front stoop with a bag of potato chips, and stood calling Holly. Yes, she came in for that.

We had a bay window in our bedroom where I put my cedar chest that Jim had given me. It was in front of the window so Holly could hop up there and look out the window. It was beautiful with an embroidered top and oak carving all around. She could sit there for hours and watch out the window. One day in her early years, she looked so sweet sitting there that I went to sit beside her and she had chewed all around the oak carving. (I was able to get a new top from Lane chests!) She chewed my glasses; she chewed a new pair of shoes. She would watch me put on panty hose and I swear she would be able to put them on if she had thumbs, but she would grab them and run with them usually on days I was rushing to get to work. One day I came home when Mom was visiting, and the rung on one of my dining room chairs was all chewed! I asked Mom if she heard Holly chewing it, and she said she thought she had a toy!

Holly would bring us presents too—from other people's houses—usually trash but one time it was a real nice plant. My neighbors saw her running with our newspaper and thought we had trained her to bring in the paper, but, no, she would get the paper and then play "Tag" with us to get it from her.

Before we had Holly, a male dog had come when I was sitting on the front porch, and he was cute and we played with him, but then he started humping things, like our arms, our legs, etc. It was disgusting, and I decided I never wanted a boy dog because of this act.

After being spayed, Holly would "hump" things—people's feet, the boys' legs if they had on sweat pants, toys, etc. I never understood it as she was a female and "fixed". Jim's Dad died. He lived in South Georgia. Our minister came to pray for us as a family before we left for the funeral. As we joined together in a circle, and he began to pray, Holly just walked around inside the circle looking at each person and all I could think of was, "Dear Lord, please don't let her start humping one of our legs!' She didn't, thank you Jesus!

Our subdivision was very new, and houses were going up all around. One of our favorite things to do (mine anyway) was to visit the houses in different phases of being built. Holly always went with us. Once we were on a dirt road and just walking in the subdivision and people on horses came by. Holly attacked the horse! She was so aggressive and protective. The horse just looked at her.

Joey loved to tease Holly and she would show her teeth and make a "rat face". We would laugh. One summer day he was getting ready to go to his part-time job at the movie theater and as he teased her, she jumped up and bit his nose! It bled and left a hole! I told him to tell his employer that he was trying a nose stud!

Holly hated taking a bath. I would take her to the bathtub in the basement as it had a shower spray that you could hold. Whenever I went down there to start the water, she knew what was coming and would jump on Jim's lap or under the bed so I couldn't catch her. When I

These two were always fooling around: Joey and Holly

Holly loved holidays. In the picture above, she received a ball cap for Easter since she liked chewing on them.

At Christmas, she would smell the presents but not bother with them.

On Christmas morning, Jim would put on his Santa hat and pass out the presents. She would wait patiently for hers.

tried to get her, she would also give me the "rat face" with teeth showing. After her bath, I would dry her well and she would run from one end of the house to the other, tearing at the towel and throwing it up in the air as if it was the towel's fault that she had a bath! Since our house had an open floor plan, sometimes she would run from the kitchen, through the living room, through the dining room, and back into the kitchen several times, as we would say, "Go Holly Go!". To finish it off or when she got too tired, she would make the circle and then from the Living Room run to our bedroom and jump up on our bed to rest. It was like her grand finale and then we would applaud! She brought so much joy to all of us.

After the boys were older, and didn't want to do things with us, I drove alone to visit my Mom, and Holly became my new copilot. One time I took her to Mom's and all the family came. My brother Harry Lee brought his wiener dog, "Twinkie" as he thought two little dogs would get along. Wrong! Holly became a maniac, and we put her in Mom's bathroom and shut the door. The little kids would put their fingers under the door, and she would nip at them and they would all scream. There was never a dull moment with my Holly.

One time Jim and I were going to be gone for a week, and Joey, who was a Senior at the University of Georgia, said he would take Holly and keep her at his apartment. I think they had a very good time together as she would sleep and look out the window while he went to school. Then he would run and take her with him. When he brought her home, and was getting ready to go back to school, he called for her to come to see if she would go again. She ran under our bed! She liked being home.

When Mom was 92, she became sick with pneumonia. Jim was traveling for his job, and I knew I needed to get there in a hurry. So, Holly

Once the boys left for college, Holly became our "empty nest" dog!

and I took off in the car for Ohio. We stayed in a little motel and I would go down in the morning and get my breakfast and bring it to my room before visiting Mom, and Holly would sit on my lap and help me eat it as I cried and held her. In the evenings, my sister Maggie and her husband, Sam, would come and walk with me as we took Holly her evening walk. We did lose Mom, my best friend, and Jim flew up for the funeral. My sister Frances asked me to come to her house while Jim was flying up, so I brought Holly and she walked on her coffee table, on her couch, and just acted like she owned the place. At least she made us laugh during a very sad time.

My mother passed away in April, and James, our oldest, was graduating from UCLA Law School in May—on Mother's Day. I had made reservations months before for us to fly out for graduation, and then drive with James and Joey to Las Vegas to celebrate. I had to take Holly to the Vet's office which also had a kennel. My heart was very heavy anyway, but when we got to the Vet's office, Holly jumped on to the top of my car hood and tried to hold on. She did not want to go there! We were gone about a week and a half, and when I returned to pick her up, Dr. Morgan said he was very worried about Holly—she wouldn't eat and looked like a puppy. After that when we would have to leave her, we hired a dog sitter who came twice a day, took her out, fed her and let her pee and she could stay in her own home.

After losing my Mom, I was very sad. I went to work, came home, put on a nightgown and just sat around, very sad. Our neighbors next door had one son, and he and his wife had just had a baby. They came over on bicycles one evening with the little baby boy on a tent-like thing on the back of the bicycle. Holly was very interested in the baby, and at first would just peek around the corner of the living room as we were introduced to him. His name was Drew, and my oldest sister had been one of the first people to hold him when he was born in Land O' Lakes, Florida. She and my neighbors' son went to the same church! Anyway, Holly slowly brought her favorite toys to the baby and was very interested in him. They stayed for a while and offered their condolences and the baby sure cheered me up. When they left, the Dad put Drew in the little wagon with a tent over it, and Holly barked and barked. She did not want them to take the baby! I think that was when I realized that a grandchild would be wonderful! However, James was starting law practice and Joey was finishing up getting his Master's so it wasn't a good time to bring up the subject! (and they weren't even married!)

Jim and I usually rode to work together unless he had to work overtime. Holly would act very sad when we left in the mornings. When we came home in the evenings, she would jump and jump for Jim (just like Tag did for Mom) and he would say, "Good Golly, Miss Holly!" She was just so precious to us. One time he worked over when we had ridden together and told me to go home and he would call me to pick him up later. It was getting pretty late, so I told Holly she could ride with me to pick up Jim. We had to stop the car at the Military Police Gate, and this dog of ours tried to take down the MP's, barking and showing her teeth while they checked my ID. We always told her if she lived until we retired, we would take her on a long vacation with us.

Several years after graduating from UCLA Law School, James accepted a position with an Atlanta law firm and moved back to Georgia from California, bringing his-wife-to be, Erin. They stayed with us a couple of days while they looked for an apartment. Erin was looking for a teaching position so she was the only one who stayed at home during the day. One day she called me at work and said she thought there was "something wrong" with Holly as she kept going to the door acting like she had to pee. I asked Erin if she was giving Holly a treat each time she came in, and she said, "Yes", and there was the answer! As I said, Holly was very smart.

James and Erin soon adopted their own dog—a real Jack Russell Terrier, and so sweet. They named her Cinnamon. She was so tiny when they first brought her to our house, I was afraid Holly would not like her since she had been "top dog" for so long. Holly didn't know what to think of her and would open her mouth on the little dog's back and just lick her and make her hair wet. They soon became friends and when Holly would pee, Cinnamon would go to the spot, smell, and pee herself. Since James and Erin were new doggie parents, they went by the book with Cinnamon, no extra treats, etc. One day I had to stay at their house to watch for the electric man, and James called me in the evening. He had found a "pretzel" in Cinnamon's food bowl. That darn dog had begged me for some of my lunch so I thought a pretzel wouldn't hurt her. Little did I know, she didn't eat it, put it in her bowl and got me in trouble!

When Jim turned 60 and I was 57, we retired. I didn't realize that I talked so much about Holly, but she even received presents from my co-workers at my retirement party. Also, when my friend Diane retired, they made her a quilt and Holly's picture was on it! Another friend from work, Theresa, always said when she died, she wanted to come back as Linda Johnson's dog so I guess I did talk about her and praise her often, and they thought she had a pampered life! We retired in November and Jim planned a 30- day car trip out West for us in May. He had it all planned ahead of time of how many miles we would travel each day, what dog-friendly hotels we would stay, and we had the time of our lives. We went from Georgia, thru Alabama, Mississippi, Louisiana, Arkansas, stopped to visit his brother in Texas, then

By the time Cinnamon came into the family, Holly was a pro posing for pictures. Joey is holding his new "dog-niece", James holding a smiling Holly and Erin — our new daughter-in-law.

One Thanksgiving, Jim went to Fort Benning and brought our great-nephew and his friend to our house for the holiday. They were so young and in training. They would get up and run in the mornings. After a big Thanksgiving meal, they were worn out, so Holly joined them for a little nap.

"Hey, don't leave me out of the picture—I helped him study!" Joey after graduating from UGA, James and Grandma Bower.

on to New Mexico, Colorado, North Dakota, Wyoming, and Montana. It was so much fun, and Holly got to go with us! She was so smart no matter what hotel floor we were on, she would watch the floor number and when the elevator bell rang for our floor, she would start for the door. She also would run down the hall to our room! She got to visit the White Sands in New Mexico, and even though it was early May, they told us to watch her paws as sometimes the sand would be too hot for dogs' paws. Jim and I climbed in Indian dwellings and up ladders and crawled through caves. I am very claustrophobic and just had to tell myself that I would never be that young again or to be able to move like that and now I am so glad I did it when I could. It was such a nice time. When we saw our first buffalo, I was very excited. They would stand in front of the truck and we had to wait for them to cross the road, but Holly would be barking for them to move. We went to Jackson Hole, Wyoming, and walked all over town. Outside one store was a stuffed buffalo, and Holly spent about ten minutes just standing there barking at it.

After Joey graduated from the University of Georgia, and then received a Master's Degree from Indiana University, he decided to go to Law School at George Washington Law School smack dab in the middle of Washington D.C.

Since we were retired, and Holly was a good travel dog, he asked us to come see him and bring Holly. He found a hotel near his apartment with a sitting room and bedroom and they accepted dogs. It did my heart good and I was so excited as we parked in front of the hotel in Jim's Dodge Truck and up the street came our youngest son, looking so grown up with a Starbucks coffee in his hand grinning from ear to ear and so happy to see—-Holly! He was so happy to see her, and there was a dog park within walking distance. Holly surprised all of us by acting very "citified" and did not bark at all the strangers on the street.

Holly was getting older when I signed up to walk her in a parade in Douglasville to help the local animal shelter. However, she wasn't always agreeable to do what I wanted her to do (like my sons), so I took my grand-dog Cinnamon instead. Everyone oohed and awed about her. She got loose from me, and I was saying, "Come here, Holly!" and some of them said, "I thought you said her name was Cinnamon." I was so embarrassed—I think they thought I just kidnapped a dog to be in the parade! Holly and I went on walks with Erin and Cinnamon in Atlanta parks too, but Holly just was not friendly and didn't do well with other dogs. She never thought she was one!

A friend of mine (Barbara) adopted a Mexican Chihuahua. She came to visit us and had her little dog trained so well. She also brought a basket with all her dog's toys in it. Holly would have nothing to do with the little Chihuahua, so he sat quietly in his Momma's lap. When Barbara got ready to leave, most of the toys were missing from her dog's basket! My Holly had one by one taken the toys and put them under my bed! My friend called her the "devil dog"!

I noticed in our local paper that the Catholic Church in Lithia Springs was going to have a "blessing of the animals" ceremony and as Holly was getting up in years, I thought this would be a good thing for her. I am Methodist so wasn't sure what the ceremony entailed. We arrived and were sent outside to a big circle of people with all kinds of animals, even iguanas and big birds. The priest came around and shook "Holy Water" on all the animals, as he blessed them. I knew that when Holly left us, she would be on the rainbow bridge waiting for us, but this just made me feel she was going there for sure. I told Jim that when the water hit Holly, it went "hisssssssss"!

Thanksgiving has always been my favorite holiday. One year, I rented a cabin in North Carolina. It was three-stories and looked out over the mountains. The owners approved of our bringing Holly and Cinnamon. Jim and I took the upstairs bedroom with a bath and large king bed. Maggie and Sam had a room of their own. Jo Anne and her daughter, Karen, had a room, and Sheryl, Maggie and Sam's daughter, got the living room sofa. James, Erin, and Joey got the basement with a pool table and several beds. We had all settled down for the night, and Holly, Jim and I were enjoying our large bed. I was asleep but Jim said all at once, he saw James crawling across our bedroom floor. He had Cinnamon with him, and said she "needed Grandma". I guess she was crying all night and the kids decided to send her to us. Since our bed was large, she and Holly, and Jim and I went back to sleep. The hardest part of being on the third floor was the mornings when we had to rush down the stairs with the two dogs so they could take their morning pee! Other than that, we all had a good time.

As Holly got older, her walks became shorter. I often thought of getting a baby carriage to push her around. We lived on a hill and I would ask her to go get the mail with me, and she would just sit on top of the hill, like, "I'll just wait here, thank you very much." She would get situated on all fours and couldn't get up, and she started having many accidents in the house. When we went outside, she would stare at the side of the house like, "Open this door!" but it wouldn't be the door. I knew her time with us was getting shorter but didn't want to think about it. I bought doggie diapers and even newborn rubber pants to put over them, but that didn't work either.

In Holly's 16th year, Jim's middle brother, Ray, who had moved to Florida, died. Jim had already been visiting him in Florida, and I flew down for the funeral. After the funeral, we went to the home to be with his children and grandchildren. I noticed a golden retriever there called Samantha "Sam". The grandchildren sat all around with their plates full of food, and the dog would just sit as close as she could to them, but not try to get their food, just looked at it drooling. I thought she was a pretty dog and well behaved but didn't think much else about it. I also thought if Holly had been there, she would have grabbed something from their plate and run with it. I came home from the funeral, and Jim came later. He called me and said that no one wanted Sam, and could he bring her home. I said, "NO!" We had agreed when Holly passed, we wouldn't get another dog so we could travel at the drop of a hat and not worry about who would watch the dog and so on. Plus, Holly was a full-time job, just keeping her cleaned up, etc. He drove home from Florida. When he arrived, he was a mess, crying, saying he needed to do something for his brother, he always wanted a big dog to take hunting and to the woods, etc., so —— I said, "OK!"

He drove back to Florida that same day and picked up Sam and came back home all in one day. She came in the house looking so big with that big, fat tail just wagging all over the place. She wagged it into Holly's eyes and Holly would just blink, as if to say, "What is this thing?" The two dogs soon became friends—Holly just lived in her own little world, and Sam would watch out for her, like when they would go outside, Sam would stop before coming in, as if to say, "where is the old dog, and is she coming in?" Sam loved to walk, and although Jim said he would walk her, she became my walking buddy and sometimes my neighbor Caroline would walk Holly while I walked Sam. Holly just didn't like to go very far. Sam just filled the whole house and would knock things off the coffee table with that big old wagging tail! She really shed more hair than Holly too!

My sister Frances visited us in the fall of that year, and Sam would go in and jump in bed with her! Frances loved her. In fact, anyone who met Sam loved her and she loved people!

Thanksgiving is always a wonderful time at our house and my favorite holiday. However, that year, we had three dogs—Holly, Sam and Cinnamon along with our visitors and the kids. I was very concerned and had to keep my eye on Holly most of the time and she was having more accidents. Jim and I talked after the holidays and decided that it was probably time to put Holly down. I even called for an appointment, and the night before neither of us could sleep. We both turned to each other the next morning and said, "I can't do it." so we agreed to cancel the appointment as we weren't ready. We just loved her so much, and it was so hard to let her go.

That Thanksgiving after getting Sam in August, was a very hard time. I was used to just letting Holly out to pee and after 16 years, she never ran away. Sam, on the other hand, was a different story. The men were watching football, and Sam went to the door to pee, so I let her out, kept talking with my sisters and sort of lost time. Jim asked where Sam was and I told him she went out to pee. When I looked for her, she wasn't out there and he got real upset, and said in front of a houseful of people, "Don't you ever let her out again on her own!" It was very awkward and embarrassing, but he did put his coat on and went out and found her.

After Thanksgiving, my sister Jo Anne and I went to Cherokee, North Carolina, to gamble for a few days. We had a good trip and came home, and Jim was glad to see us. Jo Anne was washing the lunch dishes and I let Sam out "to pee". Again, we probably talked about our trip and lost count of time, when Jim asked where Sam was! We both went out to find her, and there was no trace. Jo Anne stood at the sink, crying, as she didn't want her baby sister to get in trouble again. Something came over me, and while Jim looked out in the woods behind the house, I got in the car and left the subdivision. I was drawn to another subdivision which abutted ours, and started going down the streets to the area that came close to our subdivision. There walking down the street, big as you please, was Sam! She was just walking down the sidewalk enjoying the sights. I called to her, and even had to look at her ID tag to be sure it was her as she acted like she didn't even know me. I got her in the car and took her home to a grateful sister and quiet husband! That was a miracle to me, and I just felt that God told me to go there!

In January, Jim left with buddies to Missouri for a wild hog hunt. It was a Sunday evening and I was walking Sam and Holly when two men stopped me and looking frantic said they were not from this area, and heard a big storm was coming and they kept getting turned around in the subdivision. I directed them how to get out and back to I-20 where they could find hotels, and went on home. I watched the news and, yes, Atlanta and the outlying areas were in for a big storm. It started that evening and continued. I knew I was warm, had plenty of food and with a hunter husband had all kinds of lanterns, etc. to make it through the storm. The next morning, we awoke to a beautiful winter wonderland. The patio was deep with snow so I made a path for Holly to go to the yard to pee, and didn't worry about Sam who jumped and ran and enjoyed the snow. I let them out to do their business and made my coffee and then went out to get them. Sam was nowhere to be found, and Holly had gone down the side of the hill and was in a ditch. All I could think of was rappelling with a rope tied to one of the trees up the hill to get Holly. After much coaxing and begging her, and going down into the ditch myself, I got her out and back into the house. She had enjoyed the snow. Now to get Sam. I thought of all kinds of things, mostly screaming her name and walking in the woods. I would catch sight of her and then she would run. My kids had flute-a-phones from grade school (they call them recorders now), and I don't know what made me think of it, but I got one out and started playing it, and Sam ran home! That week the neighbor down the street would bring his Irish Setter for Sam to play with in our front yard and they would chase each other and frolic in the snow. Holly would go out but she was so over the snow in one day! We had a very cozy week alone and my only discomfort was we lost cable and couldn't watch our soaps! Oh yes, both dogs knew when it was time for "The Young and the Restless" and when the theme song would play, they would take their places on the couch and floor knowing that I wasn't moving for an hour and there might be treats! Jim came home in a week, and the both dogs were so glad to see him and acted like I was just some old lady who happened to be there.

In her day, Holly loved to play catch with a ball and would retrieve the ball over and over until the thrower was tired out. Sam would catch the ball once or twice and she was done, but our grand-dog Cinnamon would catch a ball all day. I would throw the balls to Holly and Cinnamon taking turns, and as she got older, Holly would grab the ball and walk to the door, like, "I am tired now, playtime is over." She became the old lady of the group!

Time went by quickly, and Jim would take the dogs to the walking trail in our county. He would walk miles with Sam, and I would follow with Holly. Although she always liked to walk, she was slowing down.

One day in the summer of 2011, we were gone longer than normal during the day and came home to Holly in her own mess and couldn't walk out of it. I cried and cried and told her how sorry I was as I gave her a bath and cleaned her and loved on her. Her eyes seemed to tell me that she understood. I did take her to the Vet the next day. It was so hard, and Jim couldn't go. They talked to me and told me I was doing a good thing for her, and I wouldn't want her to be frightened or alone when she died. They gave me a treat to give to her and gave her a shot. She always loved to eat, and ate the treat while I stood there and cried. Then she looked at me, and her little stub of a tail shook back and forth as if to say, "It is okay." It was so fast as one minute she was with me and then she was gone. They wrapped her up and carried her to the car, as Jim was home, getting her grave site ready. He made a box for her and we put her favorite dinosaur toy and some pictures of us in it, and buried her on the hill behind our house. We can see her grave when we look out, and he bought a stone that says, "Good friends leave footprints on your heart". She loved to go to the woods behind the house and stand there looking at us and I imagine she is still doing that.

Sam seemed sad to lose Holly. Jim continued to walk with her, and was getting her conditioned to take hunting with him. However, that Fall, instead of hunting in Georgia, he took a trip to the state of Washington to hunt Elk. Sam and I went with him and stayed in Seattle at a very nice hotel that accepted dogs, and Jim went on to the country to hunt Elk. The city of Seattle is the most dog-friendly city I have every been in. I was really dreading going because I thought it rained all the time, but the rain doesn't keep the people from taking their pets and babies outdoors all the time. There was a park across the street from our hotel so I could take Sam there first thing in the morning and the last thing at night. She would try to climb the trees after

*One romp in the snow and down a snowy ditch
was enough for this elderly girl!*

Holly always enjoyed eating. She had a good appetite until the end.

the squirrels that were prevalent there. There were also homeless people sleeping there and all over the town. The men were friendly and almost always petted and talked to Sam. The women seemed scary and one even said, "Yes, you might know she has to have the prettiest dog." I never felt scared, because Sam was with me. We walked to a "dog park" that was top notch with all kinds of things for dogs to do and climb. Sam was very shy at first and would hide behind me like a little child. However, by the end of the week, she was climbing on things and playing with other dogs. I met people from all over the country and one even had a descendent of UGGA, the English Bulldog University of Georgia mascot! We walked all over and down to Pike's Market which is amazing. A young couple was petting Sam and in talking, we found they were from Georgia too, and not far from where we lived. During the days, I would walk Sam, take her to the dog park, and then we would look for restaurants where I might like to eat. There was also a Whole Foods close by, and I would often get my lunch there and return to eat with Sam and watch our "Soaps" together. Sam was a good traveler and would just sit down in the back seat of the truck and never complain. Jim didn't get an Elk but we did run into awful weather on the way home, and he even bought snow chains for the truck. The drive home made me realize how much I appreciated the South in Winter.

Maggie and Sam have come to our house for Thanksgiving more than I can count. They started when Mom could no longer fly by herself and so they would bring her down and my sister, Jo Anne and her husband Bob, from Florida would come up. After Mom died, we kept the tradition. Even our neighbors said it wasn't Thanksgiving unless they saw Jo Anne and Bob's motor home from Florida parked in front of our house. Anyway, that Thanksgiving, Maggie and Sam, Jo Anne (Bob had died the year we retired), Erin, James, Cinnamon and Jim and Sam and I were waiting for Joey and Natalie. I think Joey took it very hard, losing Holly, and thought we brought Sam into the family and then she took Holly's place. He and his girlfriend, Natalie (now his wife), arrived from Virginia and hugged us all and then said they had a surprise in the car. We were all guessing what it could be—enter my second grand-dog, Bandit.

Bandit was so excited and so pretty. She was black and white and got along well with Cinnamon and Sam right away. However, she did like to bite on Sam's ears.

She was crate trained and would sleep in her cage at night or when they told her to get it in it! Such disciplinarians were my children! Now both sons had their own dogs! The next year after Thanksgiving, Joey went to Peru to meet his wife and her family in Peru. Bandit stayed at Grandma's and Grandpa's and with Sam. She was such an easy dog. I walked both she and Sam at the same time with no problems at all. She and Sam would play with each other. After Joey picked her up and left for Virginia, we did find scabs on poor Sam's ears where Bandit had been a little too rough. Sam just took it and never fought or bit Bandit back although she was much larger.

Sam had a knee problem—sort of like football players. She would limp. The vet sent us to many surgeons and the cost to fix the problem was so high. Jim decided to check the University of Georgia Veterinary hospital. We took Sam for a consultation. It was the most efficient, clean and pleasant place to be. I told Jim he could take me there if I ever required surgery. Sam immediately became shy when it was her turn and she ran and tried to get behind me. My heart ached. They performed the surgery and she was there a couple of days. She even walked on a treadmill in the water. Her recovery was long, and

*Aunt Jo Anne with her new "grand-niece" dog Bandit –
our Thanksgiving surprise!*

Jim had to put her in a sling to help her walk outside to go potty. He also had to "exercise her leg" so many times a day and he was a very good nursemaid. Cinnamon would also watch and so would our little grand-daughter—Yes we got one of those finally!! James and Erin had a daughter, and she loved Sam and Sam loved her. She called and still calls Cinnamon her "sister".

One Spring, Joey and Natalie scheduled a vacation in Savannah—the town Joey was born in, at the oceanside. Jim and I went to be with them the first part of the week, and Erin, James and baby Drew went the second part of the week. James, Joey and Natalie scheduled an evening to watch the dolphins and Erin and Drew stayed back at the rental. Erin said the last thing Joey told her was to take care of his dog, Bandit. Erin took Bandit and Drew out in the back yard to enjoy the weather and Bandit ran away. Erin took little Drew back in the house and left her to chase down Bandit. She said she knew Joey would kill her if she lost that dog. It all turned out okay.

Joey and Natalie adopted another dog—her name was Monkey. Monkey was very nervous and didn't like too many people. Her sweet little face and body reminded me of Holly. Joey and Natalie were going to leave Monkey and Bandit with me and my company while they went to an over-night trip to a Georgia game after Thanksgiving. Natalie told me when it was bedtime to tell them to get in their cage. I thought, "Right, I can see this happening." My sister, Maggie, and I always stayed up late talking and I said, "Ok, girls, time to get in your cage for bedtime." They did! They actually got in their cage and wrapped around each other for the night! I told Maggie they were sisters like us, and said I hope when Joey and Natalie had children, they would mind so well!

Another story about Monkey, which I thought was hilarious was when Natalie dressed both dogs for Halloween and took them to their local neighborhood's Halloween activities. Long story short, the crowds and people scared Monkey and she ran from Natalie. Natalie was beside herself looking for Monkey, when a lady stopped her car and asked if Natalie was looking for a "Lady Bug". It was Monkey who Natalie had dressed as a Lady Bug. Joey and Natalie now have a daughter, and I tease Natalie about the "Lady Bug", and not to lose my Granddaughter Gwendolyn Elise!

Joey and Natalie invited us to Alexandria, Virginia, for Christmas one year, and since Jim didn't want to leave Sam, they said Sam was invited too. We had a wonderful time, tour of the decorated White House, a play, "White Christmas" at the Kennedy Center, just so many interesting things to do and see. Sam was okay, but after that visit, I vowed to leave her at the kennel if we ever went back. They had visiting family and friends, and Sam had to be the center of attention, and I realized that it isn't fun for the hosts or other guests to bring your dog along.

Joey and Natalie moved to Switzerland after they were married in 2014. Jim and I along with many family and friends attended their beautiful wedding in Alexandria, Virginia and the reception at the Mason Hall! We enjoyed all the festivities, but with a heavy heart knew we would soon be seeing them depart for Switzerland the following week. They had movers and packers in, and our job was to deliver fast food to them all. They were so tense and nervous about their dogs' flight as it would be on the same plane as they took. Our job was to get their crates and the dogs to the airport. I talked to the Monkey and Bandit the whole time and told them I would see them again and to love my boy and Natalie, and my heart was aching for my baby son, just as it did when we left James in California. Lives and people change! Natalie's parents were at the airport to say good-bye too, but our children didn't hang on our necks or cry because they were leaving us—they were concerned for their poor babies having to fly that long! I understood.

I did make the trip to Switzerland a year and a half later, leaving Jim and Sam at home. I think Monkey and Bandit remembered me. I had a wonderful time with the kids, and I think I liked Italy best where we stayed for a couple of days in Tuscany region. We enjoyed wine tastings and visited Florence where we looked down at the town as our guide told us we would be walking down there. I was so glad that I had kept walking with Sam to prepare me for walking all day. It was wonderful.

In December of 2017, our whole family went to Switzerland. James and Erin had to leave Cinnamon with someone, and we had to board Sam. I was so sad to take her to the kennel. I told my sister Frances that if something happened to Jim and I to have our brother Charlie—yes that ornery brother—get Sam out of the kennel and take her home to live with he and his wife Tami. They have a wonderful pet farm with horses, goats, chickens, dogs, cats, miniature donkeys and now he has a pet pig too! As I said at the beginning, I think our parents encouraged our love for animals. His farm is another book altogether.

Our Christmas visit to Switzerland was to visit with and get acquainted with our new granddaughter, Gwendolyn, who was born in November of 2017! So now from two ornery boys, I have two perfect grand-daughters. We had a good time meeting Gwendolyn and were so glad to see our grand-dogs too. Monkey and Bandit had flourished in Switzerland and did lots of hiking in the Alps.

They were so concerned about getting Monkey and Bandit to Switzerland healthy and safe that they didn't worry about both sets of parents whose hearts were breaking at losing their "babies"!

Taking my "grand-dog" Monkey and Bandit on a walk in Switzerland.
These dogs are more world-traveled than their Grandma!

Our family was complete — from two ornery sons—
two perfect granddaughters.

We had Sam as our only dog for a while. She was known all around the subdivision as I walked her daily. She is just a loveable dog. Jim's youngest brother got sick. He had throat cancer, and Jim went to Texas to care for him in his own home. When Jim would call me in the evenings, I would hear a dog barking constantly. I asked him what was wrong with it, and he said that it was Lucky and he barked all the time. He lived with Jim's brother and stayed outside all day and in the garage at night. Jim stayed with his brother several months and then came home and went back again. It was hard on him, but he loved his brother and it kept his brother staying in his own home. The last time Jim came home from his brother's, he brought Lucky with him. I knew he was used to being outside so I put a gate up between the kitchen and the rest of the house and thought he could start out there. After a long ride from Texas, Jim came in with the biggest male dog. He immediately went over to the gate in the kitchen, hiked his leg and peed on it. In my kitchen! Then when Sam came out, he tried to mount her! Oh no, what were we thinking taking in another dog???

I felt sorry for this big dog too. One ear was torn! He slept in the laundry room several nights and would go out to potty when Sam did. Little by little, Sam and he became friends. We took down the divider from the kitchen and Lucky became an "inside dog". We had recently had beautiful hardwoods put down, but then Jim became concerned for the dogs and bought carpets. Our house looks like we are having a carpet sale. Now instead of one large cage in the master bedroom, there are two, with two plush lounges for dogs in the Living Room, one under the window in our bedroom. Needless to say, the dogs have the run of our house. Jim had bought me a robot vacuum with Sam's arrival. Now I have two and they could run day and night as there is hair everywhere.

Lucky will shake but only with his left hand. I tell people that is because he is from Texas. Lucky loved our granddaughter, Drew. We were careful at first because we do not know his background.

Jim and I had a routine on Friday or Saturday nights, we would go for Mexican food and he would have margaritas, and I would drive home. One evening, as we were on our way to our favorite Mexican Restaurant, we got a call that the home alarm was going off. Jim said for them to turn it off as it was probably one of the dogs barking setting it off. We went, had a good meal, Jim had his margaritas and came home to phone calls and email from the neighborhood. Seems as if the front door was wide open and the alarm went off for 30 minutes. The front door was wide open, and Lucky was running the neighborhood. One man in the neighborhood was going to come inside to see if we were ok, but was afraid Jim would be inside and shoot him for coming in. Sam stayed inside during this period, but Lucky ran all over. Finally, our good neighbor, Mike Johnson, whistled for him and he came and Mike put him in the house and closed the door.

The arrival of Lucky

Drew. We were careful with him around her at first because we do not know his background. When Drew visits, Lucky is her shadow!

Thank God for good neighbors. One neighbor told me they wanted to call the sheriff (we are the oldest people on the street and they probably thought one of us had perished) but then they were afraid the sheriff would come and shoot the dog! Oh My God—and we were just thinking all was right with the world and having a nice meal! We realized living with Lucky wasn't going to be as easy as our other dogs.

Our subdivision is rolling hills, and I was aging and walking the hills was not as easy as it used to be. The high school less than a mile away has sidewalks all around and is a good, level walking place. I started putting Sam, Lucky and Cinnamon (if she was visiting) in the car and taking them there to walk. I would unleash them if no one was around and we would walk all over and then return to the car and home. The dogs loved it. The first time taking Lucky, he came from the back seat to the front and had to sit up front like a big old man! It was funny.

This went on very well and I was still getting my much-needed walks in for myself and taking the dogs too. One day I had parked and was walking in front of the High School when I saw our neighbor boy approaching us. He was a friendly boy and had his cellphone on and was talking. For some reason, Lucky went berserk, pulled on the leash and was so powerful, I had to let him go or fall down. Then because Lucky was barking and going crazy, Sam began to bark too! Lucky knocked the phone out of my neighbor's hand and pulled his low-riding pants off. I thought I might have a stroke. The neighbor was young and agile, and handed me Lucky's leash and he went on, and I had to calm my dogs down and get them in the car. I told this to Jim and said that I couldn't walk both dogs ever again.

I knew I couldn't just walk Sam and leave Lucky behind, so I just had to walk alone. It made me very sad, but Jim started walking both dogs

Of course, Lucky wouldn't stay in the back seat with the "girls"! He had to show he was the "man of the group" getting in the front seat. I think he would have driven if he knew how. Sam and Cinnamon didn't mind.

in the woods behind us so they were getting their exercise but I still needed to get mine—alone!! I still would take them both out to get the mail with me, with Lucky always on a leash. One time just as we came out of the garage Lucky saw the little dog across the street with one of his owners walking in their own yard! Lucky pulled me so hard, I again had to let go of the leash and screamed at the boy, "Pick up your dog! Pick up your dog!" Lucky was running so fast. The young man picked up his dog and ran inside. I had to tell Lucky I can't take him anywhere even in the front yard on a leash as he is too strong for me. I called the young man's parents and apologized and told them I wouldn't be bringing Lucky into the front yard ever. I asked if their dog was okay, and my neighbor said the little dog was just walking all over the house saying, "Let me at him! Let me at him!"

In 2019, Jim and I were summoned once again to the Airport in D.C. to pick up our grand-dogs. Joey and family had come home! It was such a nice homecoming, and the best part was being with little Gwendolyn. Monkey and Bandit were glad to see us too! They had come full circle and were ready to go to their home in Virginia.

Before the trip to pick up the kids at the airport, we had to get Lucky accepted at the kennel. Lucky had serious temperament issues, so the head of the kennel told one of the workers to take Lucky and put him in with Ole Blue. We heard lots of barking and growling and finally she walked out with Lucky and said, "Lucky attacked Ole Blue right away." Poor Ole Blue—I guess he was the test dog for aggressiveness. Anyway, they said they would board Lucky but he wouldn't be in the regular area with Sam.

Once the Pandemic arrived, Sam and Lucky became even more dear to us since we couldn't go anywhere. Thanksgiving 2020—Our son

Christmas at our house. Jim still puts on the Santa hat and, of course, the dogs receive their presents first!

Joey, his wife Natalie, Gwendolyn and their two dogs, Bandit and Monkey, came for Thanksgiving. Maggie and Sam who usually come didn't because of COVID. James and Erin and Drew came for the day but didn't stay all night. I had put that divider out again to divide "their dogs" from "our dogs". It was pleasant weather and when we were outside (in the back), the dogs seemed to get along okay except Monkey who has issues. We still kept Lucky and Sam in one part of the house and Monkey and Bandit in the other part. After Dinner, Bandit got curious and came into the living room by bypassing the gate and going through the Dining Room. I guess Lucky was sitting by Jim at the time and upon seeing Bandit (who is so good natured and loving like Sam) approaching them, Lucky attacked Bandit! I was at the dining room table at the time and just prayed. Lots of barking, screaming, etc. I guess James who was on the couch jumped up and tackled Lucky, getting him off Bandit and Joey and Natalie rushed in to administer to Bandit.

Well, this sums up our life til now. We have lived through the pandemic, have our vaccines, still don't go out in crowds, and still have Sam and Lucky who are both about eleven. I often think of the places we could have seen and gone without Sam and Lucky, but they were such a comfort the past year when we just had to stay here. They love us and we love them, and my house will never be the neat place that I was born to have, but I guess that isn't everything. Again, my Mom and Dad let us bring animals in the house and I owe my love of all animals to them. God bless my family, friends and all the animals.

Joey, Gwendolyn, Bandit and Monkey

*Lucky didn't understand that this Tea was for Grandma
and her beautiful Granddaughters.*

Sam and Lucky enjoyed the story Joey read to Gwendolyn!

During the pandemic, Drew had to go to "virtual school", She wanted to stay with us overnight, and I was very nervous about her getting on line and attending school. She was fine with it, and her parents were too so she came. My sons, James and Joey, have a sense of humor that always got them out of trouble with me when they were growing up, and I think Drew is developing that same humor. After each class, she would have a break, and then on to another subject. I was going on about my business, thinking everything was okay when Drew told me to "Come Quick!". She had put her earphones on Sam and put the computer in front of her. She said that Sam was taking that class for her!

When this picture was taken at Thanksgiving, I didn't realize that our newest dog, Ahsa Rose, was there. I think she is trying to help get Thanksgiving dinner on the table.

Drew and her rescue dog, Ahsa Rose.

I often thought of wearing roller skates
and letting them pull me on our walks

James and his "big brother"

Happy Easter—yes, they were bribed with a treat for this picture!

Old folks at home